KINGS OF THE GREEN JELLY MOON
The Book, Volume 1.5

Lloyd King, jim greenwald,
James Jellerson, and Mike Mullins

iUniverse, Inc.
Bloomington

Kings of the Green Jelly Moon
The Book, Volume 1.5

Copyright © 2011 Lloyd King, jim greenwald, James Jellerson, and Mike Mullins

All rights reserved. No part of this book may be used or reproduced by any means, graphic, electronic, or mechanical, including photocopying, recording, taping or by any information storage retrieval system without the written permission of the publisher except in the case of brief quotations embodied in critical articles and reviews.

iUniverse books may be ordered through booksellers or by contacting:

iUniverse
1663 Liberty Drive
Bloomington, IN 47403
www.iuniverse.com
1-800-Authors (1-800-288-4677)

Because of the dynamic nature of the Internet, any Web addresses or links contained in this book may have changed since publication and may no longer be valid. The views expressed in this work are solely those of the author and do not necessarily reflect the views of the publisher, and the publisher hereby disclaims any responsibility for them.

Any people depicted in stock imagery provided by Thinkstock are models, and such images are being used for illustrative purposes only.

Certain stock imagery © Thinkstock.

ISBN: 978-1-4620-2789-7 (sc)
ISBN: 978-1-4620-2790-3 (hc)
ISBN: 978-1-4620-2791-0 (e)

Printed in the United States of America

iUniverse rev. date: 6/6/2011

Other Works by the Poets/Authors

<u>jim greenwald</u>

Wishing for Rain
Mitakuye Oyasin
With Pen & Feather
Seen From An Open Window
Across the Bridge
[2008 Gold Medal Award]
Sugar, Zeroes & Lemon Drops
[Bronze Medal 2009]
Tears for Mother Earth
[2009 Gold Medal Award]
Twisted Tongues
[2010 Gold Medal Award]
Kings of the Green Jelly Moon [CD]
[2010 Silver Medal Award]

<u>Mike "Moon" Mullins</u>

VietNam in Verse: Poetry for Beer Drinkers
[2007 Gold Medal Award & 2010 Gold Medal for Audio Book]
Kings of the Green Jelly Moon [CD]
[2010 Silver Medal]

Lloyd King

From 'Nam with Love
[2006 Gold Medal Award]
Kings of the Green Jelly Moon [CD]
[2010 Silver Medal]

James Jellerson

Just for Jocks (& the People That Love Them)
Limericks, Lyrics, Riddles 'n Rhymes (The Best of Times)
Made in America: The Chameleon (series part 1)
Poems of Passion & Songs for the Soul
[2009 Silver Medal Award]
Who Am I? Who Does God Say I Am?
At the Water's Edge [Chapbook]
Perspectives [Chapbook]
Reflections of Mind [Chapbook]
The Poetry of Lyrics
Kings of the Green Jelly Moon [CD]
[2010 Silver Medal]
Through the Years

Music CDs
From the Heart
Goin' Home
Matthew James
One Way Home
The Best of Family
Sailing Away
[2010 Silver Medal]

The title *Kings of the Green Jelly Moon* is reflective of
the innocence of childhood, back to the time when
children believed the moon to be made of green cheese.
Beliefs, when confronted with reality, soon turned to truth
and so Nam changed an innocent generation as it
became immersed in the truth of war and its realities.

Vietnam cast a long shadow upon this nation. Our Constitution is a great and significant document in history. In it is called for the control of the military by the President, this done as a precaution and to protect the liberty of all in a just society.

Every good has a downside to some degree. Korea and Vietnam are the living historical proof of that. One can easily argue either side but here we will deal with the realities of results. President Truman stopped his general from advancing past the Yalu River and we all are aware of the consequences of that decision in today's political and military realities.

In Vietnam politicians took it to the next level. Fighting a war with rules put in place by people in armchairs thousands of miles away, safe in their homes has consequences. Free from the fears and terrors of war it is easy if not intentional to place others' lives in jeopardy.

War by its very nature cannot be fought with rules. This book is simply an effort to relate the emotional reality of the experiences and feelings one does not learn from Hollywood hype. It is also an attempt awaken the next generation into the "not glamorous (if there were any) side" of war and hopefully touch an emotional chord to the realities of war as it is remembered. We are not trying to justify Vietnam, a war in which many people feel we should never have been involved.

colored cloth

this flag of ours – no advertisement-
this multicolored cloth waving in the wind-
not some decoration to be worn on one's body-
not a trinket possessed and forgotten.

"Old Glory" yesterday, today, and tomorrow,
her seeds of hope spread to all,
this colored cloth that speaks of freedom for all;
born from blood, nurtured in sweat and tears.

within her nurturing folds
dreams become reality
solemnized through sacrifice
she fuels our innocence and purity.

both flag and blanket
providing shelter and warmth
she dresses the wounds of hatred
and provides a silent dignity.

colors clear and defined
as is her mission to all but the blind
her colors not blended…her people so…
one nation – red – white – and blue.

Contents

Wishing I Could Not See	jim greenwald
Isn't It Strange	James Jellerson
A Young Soldier's Fancy	Mike Mullins
First Kill	Lloyd King
Why Speak into the Wind	jim greenwald
Combat Veteran's Perspective	Lloyd King
One by One	James Jellerson
Warriors Fraternity	Mike Mullins
Not Me	jim greenwald
Evil Song	Lloyd King
Innocence Gone	James Jellerson
Comfort Zone	Mike Mullins
Never Knew	jim greenwald
Inner Preludes	Lloyd King
Seven Stars	James Jellerson
An Asian Moon	Mike Mullins
Mist of Time	jim greenwald
On Memorial Day	Lloyd King
When the Cannons Cease	James Jellerson
Where Were You	Mike Mullins
Three for War	jim greenwald
Highest Tradition	James Jellerson
Memories	Lloyd King
Shock and Awe	Mike Mullins
Did You Know	jim greenwald
Purple Hearts	Lloyd King
The Stone	James Jellerson
The Bunker	Mike Mullins
Open Wounds	jim greenwald
Reality	Lloyd King
The Art of War	James Jellerson

Sounds	Mike Mullins
Reflections	Lloyd King
Dream in Black	jim greenwald
Final Muster	James Jellerson
The Sniper	Lloyd King
Preparation	Mike Mullins
'Til Now Unwritten	jim greenwald
The Honored Dead	James Jellerson
The Wall	Lloyd King
Slave to a Purpose	Mike Mullins
Heroes All	jim greenwald
No Cease-Fire	James Jellerson
To a Gold Star Mother	Lloyd King
What of Safe	jim greenwald
My Turn, My Tour	Mike Mullins
Unfaded Memories	jim greenwald
Put me in, Coach	Mike Mullins
Dreams - Nightmares	jim greenwald
To My Son	Lloyd King
Poet or Warrior	Mike Mullins
Headed Home	James Jellerson
Not Forgotten	jim greenwald
True Americans	Lloyd King
Let Things Go	Mike Mullins
Between	jim greenwald
Dear John	James Jellerson
Unscripted	Lloyd King
A Matter of Trust	Mike Mullins
Illusive Peace	jim greenwald
What Was I Thinking	James Jellerson
Afraid to Sleep	Mike Mullins
Veterans Day	Lloyd King
Knights of the Night	James Jellerson

Thin Wall	James Jellerson
Sleeping with Ghosts	Mike Mullins
Flag Day	Lloyd King
Honey, Me and My PTSD are Home	jim greenwald
It Don't Mean Nuthing	James Jellerson
Silence	Mike Mullins
Just Stopped By	jim greenwald

Wishing I Could Not See

The air is different here.
Tension clings to you like
a glove two sizes too small.
I try not looking into their
eyes…for fear of seeing their
terror, their fear.
Loud noises causing panic in
their reactions, indecision in
their movements.
The intermixed smells of fear
and death invade the pores of
the body, leaving an unsettled feeling.
Sleep comes far more easily
than rest…if at all.
At times thoughts turn to later,
to home, and what it would be
like now to be there.
Thoughts quickly banished from
the mind if one wants to stay
sharp…stay alive.
Combat is only a game before
you become a teenager.
Then you die for real.

Isn't It Strange

Lord, I was born into a poor home.
I grew up quick, I was left alone.
It hurt inside…isn't it strange?
I became a soldier and picked up a gun.
I was moving around having lots of fun,
'til the killing began…isn't it strange?
Remember in school, the Golden Rule
"Do unto others; don't judge a book by its cover
or a man by his skin"…isn't it strange?
Black and white, yellow and red,
killing each other over words that were said.
Such a child's game…isn't it strange?
The world today is like a child at play,
country killing neighbor because
they never learned to say, "Maybe I'm wrong."
Isn't it strange?
They don't like us, we don't like them,
let's push the button, bring our world to an end.
We'll spend eternity…together as one.

A Young Soldier's Fancy

When the night allowed any luxury
It was a folded, smelly, flak jacket
'Neath his weary head
Covered by a silky poncho liner
On the ground, damp and clammy wet.
Mother Earth was his bed.
The young soldier's fancy sailed home,
His future e'er and always the same to him,
Including the car he'd have.
College or a good job were in the dream,
The open arms of a round-eyed girl too…
A welcome from a home he left.
Each night when Lady Luck on him smiled and
A young soldier laid, arms folded, eyes upward,
Visiting his naïve dreamland.
When he boarded that Silver Bird, made the trip,
And had one of those things come true, Hoorah!
I guess one out of three ain't bad!

First Kill

[5/24/68]

I was a squad leader and I'd only been in the jungle eleven days.
A fully trained buck sergeant, but feeling lost in so many ways.
I couldn't stop shaking and my heart was pounding in my chest
Knowing that I had to prove myself worthy, like passing a test.

We'd been humping in the steep mountains ever since I arrived.
The company had been in a firefight and most of them survived.
But, after the firefight, there were only six men left in my squad.
Everyone said it was a miracle they were alive…an act of God.

Two were wounded seriously and two others had tragically died.
The survivors had to pull the weight of ten, as the order implied.
I was a nervous wreck finding out about my squad's recent fate.
New replacements was a moot issue, we'd simply have to wait.

Stand-to was at 0600, and unbelievably I was told we had point.
Fast Eddie, my automatic rifleman, promptly rolled another joint
Then informed me he couldn't function unless he was on a high.
I told him "No," took his hash, and thought he was going to cry.

I decided to walk point knowing I had personal issues to prove.
I struggled forward, but the dense jungle made it tough to move.
  I kept climbing the steep slope until I finally reached the crest
Soaked with sweat, breathing heavy, burning pains in my chest.

I signaled halt…spread the guys out, so I could recon a clearing.
I didn't like the eerie feeling and unknown sounds I was hearing.
A peculiar odor was permeating the air making me very uneasy.
My nerves were on edge…stomach in knots…and I felt queasy.

Scanning the clearing I saw something in my peripheral vision.
I turned quickly and spotted the VC, requiring a quick decision.
I yelled, "Dung yen," meaning "don't move," repeatedly to the VC
But when he reached for his rifle, I knew it would be him or me.

I stood, face-to-face, staring at my very first Vietcong guerrilla.
He was a short, skinny kid and had skin the color of pure vanilla
Wearing long, black pants and shirt which were worn and tattered,
But in that fleeting second of my life, only one thing mattered.

I crouched down fast, squeezed the trigger and fired three rounds.
My slack man reacted instinctively and responded to the sounds,
Spun around quickly, as he fired his grenade launcher or M-79.
His single round hit the VC in the gut a split second after mine.

I'd never seen a person shot before or blood and flesh splatter.
I watched in complete horror as his tiny body began to shatter.
His left bicep, right knee, and abdomen mutilated beyond belief,
I stood frozen, totally shocked, feeling a deep, emotional grief.

My grenadier and squad were all smiles, patting me on the back,
I tried to settle the guys down because I was afraid of an attack,
But nothing else happened so we began digging in for the night.
Yet, all I could think about was his body and the horrible sight.

After my squad was squared away I had to confront my anguish.
Wondering if he was married with kids and if he had a last wish,
I couldn't leave him lying there without burying him properly.
His death was strictly personal and again between him and me.

I got out my trenching tool, pretending to go and relieve myself,
But instead, I solemnly dug a grave rather than thinking of self.
While I was digging, the tears began to flow until I couldn't see.
Yet still I asked angrily, "Why the hell didn't you listen to me?"

I dug a trench and covered the bottom with big palmetto leaves
And carefully placed his body in the grave adjusting his sleeves,
I straightened both legs, then folded both arms across his chest
Telling him under the circumstances I was doing my very best.

I told him that he was the first enemy I had ever seen or killed
And tried to explain to him his fate had apparently been willed.
I recited the Lord's Prayer then I read the Twenty-Third Psalm
And when finished felt relief, but knew I'd have no inner calm.

Walking back to my squad I kept seeing his expressionless look.
The empty look I'd seen vividly with each round his body took.
I'll never forget his cold stare or how bullets hitting flesh sound,
Nor ever forget the sight of his blood soaking the fertile ground.

My very first kill remains indelible because of how it took place.
Staring into my enemy's cold eyes for the first time, face-to-face,
Knowing I had to take a life or lose mine, neither willing to give,
Both of us proud, infantry soldiers, and both determined to live.

I spent the night building his cross and at daybreak set it in place.
Then quietly spent some time with him, part of my morning grace.
I apologized to him for taking his life and being where I had been.
I saluted his grave, said he had been brave then said a final Amen.

why speak into the wind

there is a blackness that surrounds me,
an ebony shell that holds the world at bay
in some perverted logic.

within the core of my being
there are memories that twist
the core of each nerve.

the rawness of the emotion creates
a sense of drowning
here…awash in my memories.

objective thought a waste,
at best dubious, nothing attained…
the world cannot see inside of me.

there are realities and questions,
pains, sorrows, and wishes for memory loss…
questioning the whys, questioning the answers.

advice I do not need…suck it up, a waste…
how little they see, much less hear…
if only someone really cared.

blood-filled dreams, napalmed bodies…
pick up the pieces of friends in an orange rain…
walk away and be pleased ~ could you remain sane?

Combat Veteran's Perspective

Let us not forget
those who served.
Let us not forget
Recognition deserved.
Let us not forget
Freedoms that are cherished
Nor forget
Those who served
And those who perished.

One by One

Today I sit with bittersweet
Recollection of that fall,
Their faces I know, forever engraved.
All their names …I no longer can recall,
Side by side we all stood, when the day first begun
Sharing our hopes, our joys, and dreams.
By night we lay shattered, victims of truth,
Our bodies, broken and torn at the seams,
And as the smoke cleared, the stillness of night
Sighed a relief, with the setting sun.
Crimson rivers ran deep, through once green valleys.
A nation's wealth, spent one by one,
The hills we climbed, that hallowed ground,
Are now graveyards, unmarked without stone.
So many children, sent so far away,
So many lifetimes, now without a home.
We were young, we were strong, so invincible,
A generation of heroes unborn.
Our ideals, our principles, our purpose to be,
Now left with those who would mourn.
If there be victory, what price do we pay?
Wherein lies the glory to say, "We've Won"
If a nation that prides itself in wealth
Spends its greatest treasures, one by one.

Warriors Fraternity

Those who sent us did not have the courage
To let us succeed in what they asked us to do.
A spider web is life's strongest material.
Nothing else is its equal in creation.
Scientists consider only Mother Nature.
None study the bond of the soldier.

War's tribulations have been shouldered
In harm's way, in darkness, rain, and fear.
There is an inexplicable link weaved
Defying words, handshakes, and years.

Gatherings of those who shared the life
Know the strength of that unseen bond.
Years apart are only moments in passing,
When the warriors fraternity reunites.

We had the heart to engage an enemy and
The humor to laugh away the pain of duty.
We have the need to gather when we can.
Together we remember in fleeting solemnity.
We know what we did and could have done,
And those stories remain on memory's shore.

Wyatt, Weil, Brooks, Brown, Bales,
Lato, Mullins, Robinson, Gascon, Dale…
And all the rest we salute while we gather…
Names of boys who became men in that place.

As the movie says:
For we were soldiers once, and young.

Not Me

Bright, cheerful, full of purpose they
walk into the sun.
Sure of what they are doing…
sure of their mission.
Thoughts of glory replaced in a flash
by the reality of war.
Body bags on the tarmac,
a reality check for all.
A look…sorrow wells up inside for them…
for their families.
Quickly banished from the mind, it won't
happen to me, I will be more careful…more alert.
Get my tour over and home, no time to think
about the bodies on the tarmac, now but a distant memory.
Daily slogging through jungle terrain takes all your
concentration, danger exists everywhere.
Staying alert wears you down.
Time rolls on, soon it will be time to
leave…to return to sanity.
Bright, cheerful, full of purpose they
walk into the sun.
Sure of what they are doing…
sure of their purpose.
I am going home.
I wonder if that soldier walking by
notices me in this bag.
I am going home.

Evil Song

[5/16/68]

The song in my dream plays notes that are full of sorrow.
The song played last night and may play again tomorrow.
This song violates my privacy of black and white dreams
And turns gentle waters into crimson, blood-filled streams.

Streams that once sparkled crystal clear now full of death.
Their agony, quickly suffocating each bodies last breath.
The sounds of the song make me stop and make me realize
That I have so much to learn, that I'm far from being wise.

Shifting positions and ebbing like the tides of my thought,
Changing in a moment those believing life can be bought,
I tried in vain to convince myself the song really can't be
Like a hidden disease attacking the heart of a dying tree.

I will fight the song's sorrow the way I've always fought
For self-preservation and sanity hoping I'm never caught.
The song has an evil tone, a bad spirit with a broken note,
Full of eerie crescendos like a never-ending odious quote.

The song in my dream is uppermost in my sleeping mind.
Within my subconscious each note haphazardly entwined,
The song was written long ago, but now it's playing to me.
I swear to God I will resist the evil; I will never set it free.

Soon I'll be fighting in a war filled with blood and sorrow.
I hear the song now, and I hope it doesn't play tomorrow.

Innocence Gone

At fifteen
Baseball cards,
Pick-up games in backyards,
All day Saturday at the beach with friends.

At sixteen
Friday nights,
After the game showing your girl the lights,
And movie matinees that never end.

Seventeen
Step forward,
Family vacation by the lake at Castaic,
Going to San Diego to do my basic.

Overseas
A party,
At home friends at parties "throwing up"
While I responded to "Corpsman up."

High School scene
Simple dreams,
Friends looking into eyes of green, blue and fair,
I gazed into eyes that reflected only the death stare.

Party on
Time is gone,
Friends worry, don't get caught, get home safe to bed,
I worry, don't get caught, stay alive, get home instead.

Journey home
War is done,
Still the memories continue to linger on,
Won't be the same, too much pain, and innocence now gone.

Comfort Zone

Even in a war zone every soldier needs a refuge.
Somewhere there is a place that is a comfort zone.
That place is where we withdraw from the deluge.
It is where they and their dreams are safely alone.
It takes on many forms and others do not define it.
There they drag their souls out of war's black pit.

It may be a bunker, or just some cardboard shack.
Perhaps it is a tree keeping the sun off their backs;
A poncho rolled under a head, face covered in steel;
A secluded place where they have a solitary meal;
It is that soldier's space, his own place of solitude.
There is no war there, only thoughts of peace abide.

If reality comes crashing through the invisible wall
They are reminded again that there really is a war.
The whistle of a rocket overhead is a miss for sure.
The blast in your face is never the same as before.
Each time is closer; the refuge may be destroyed.
Rebuild it; don't give in; keep the spirits buoyed.

Rockets, mortars, snipers, and bombs of all kinds,
Shatter the hell out of every comfort zone, in time.
They must be encouraged for the warrior's sanity.
In a war zone nothing else is such a place of clarity.
Dig out, dig in; retrieve that place, that sanctuary.
It may be more important than the guns they carry.

Never Knew

I never knew
> how painful war was
> how senseless killing is
> how pointless it is

I never thought
> how the enemy's mom must feel
> how the enemy's children would fair
> how I would deal with the emotions—
> realities

I came to care
> how things...lives intermeshed
> how others felt
> how I could help

I came to kill
> the enemy
> to win the war
> to survive

I never knew there is only one victor in war

~ Advantage DEATH ~

Inner Preludes

[4/30/68]

Minds lifted skyward by silver wings
Soon to experience life altering things
Far away from home across an ocean
Bemused without the slightest notion.

Blank stares pierce portholes into space
Provoking thoughts of a foreign place
Reflecting silently about leaving home
Mirrored by thoughts of feeling alone.

Wings slice vapors shielding cobalt blue
Spanning the horizons in varying hue
Touching minds with chaotic emotion
Accelerated by times unseen motion.

Grooved treads kiss the steaming tarmac
While visions of a yearlong bivouac
Cross their subconscious, unconsciously
Watching others leaving…enviously.

Individuals cast randomly into their roles
Surviving one of their primary goals
Mired in questions with hearts throbbing
With forlorn hope and silent sobbing.

Stealing glances at each incredible scene
Haunted by the things yet to be seen
Heckled insensitively by soldiers leaving
Morbidly compounding inner grieving.

Pallid faces of soldiers staring curiously
Absorbing images nonsanctimoniously
Opening eyes to things, before now, surreal
Once verbalized, but sounding so unreal.

Rows and rows of black, tagged, body bags
Induce queasy feelings and a few gags
Consciously witnessing the reality of war
Training thoughts meaningless before.

Soldiers frozen in place gripped by fear
Starting day one of their combat year
Hoping prayers for continued life are heard
So they, too, will board a Freedom Bird.

Seven Stars

I still remember each of them
Their faces fill my dreams,
Three decades have since come and gone
Just yesterday, so it seems.
There was Pecos, Babe, Bronx, Philly, and J.C.,
Tooter, High-Fi, Stretch, Motown, and me.
We were solid as a rock
When our tour first began
But only three of us would ever
See our homeland again.
Tooter was the first to go
While on patrol he found a mine,
Then Pecos took a mortar round.
Direct hit…not much left to find,
Then Stretch one day, saved us all
But he paid the ultimate price.
Two weeks later in some hand-to-hand
Bronx stopped a bayonet twice.
High-Fi, Babe, and Philly one ambush…
Took the first burst and fell,
Leaving Motown, J.C., and me
To return home with the story to tell.
Late at night when the sky is dark and blue
And the stars in the heavens are bright
I find the seven…that twinkle down at me
And I thank them, and I bid them…goodnight.

An Asian Moon

The word drifted back that soon
We would stop and bivouac for the night.
An outpost would not be my job.
The seasoned soldiers would not trust me.
I would get my turn on watch, true.
It was a big test for a brand new grunt too.

Chow was a C-rat, not my first.
I was a product of Tiger Ridge, Infantry.
This was my fate, this nasty place, an Asian moon.
I was nineteen and very, very green,
A young soldier just arrived on the scene.

New to the sounds and smells of jungle
The sights and fears, questions and paddies
Of Vietnam, a place so remote to me
That it was not real even though I tasted it.
Four days into it reality began to reek.
Sweat and pain began to take over in me.

I suddenly began to look it in the face.
That first patrol, the first march into what?

An unknown was revealing itself then.
Jungle-laden hills, ants, leeches, said hello.
A stench of rotted vegetation wafted
Upward to my nostrils, sounds of things
Revealed themselves and questions…
Ah, the questions began to erupt at last.

Smiles and suggestions to do as told
Were often the only response I received.
There was not any time for chatter.
Chopping through jungle is not the place.
Silence is a weapon…and a defense.
Staring into shadows listening for sounds
That meant nothing and everything
In a classroom where days seemed eternal.

Whispered words, muted cussing, setting sun,
Mosquitoes buzzing grimy faces,
Young grunts were doing what must be done.

The sun set red, then went pink.
The sky had been damned bright all day.
Sunlight streamed in broken lines.
The jungle only revealed it in small chunks.
Camp was at its edge on one side.
There was a sky not unlike the one at home.

What a surprise that was to me.
Would the Asian moon be the same as mine?

A hand woke me at an ungodly time.
"Where was I?" was the question I did not ask.
Crawling to post it was my turn now.
I would be awake and alert, and prove myself.
Trust is earned so it can be given.
Big things are the little things done quietly.
Watch others' backs and be there.
A soldier does not have to say it or ask it.
He just knows, and it must be so.
If he can't feel it, it is the same damned way.
The night is black and scary.

The moon rises slowly and is smoky too.
When it comes will it be yellow?
What color will it be tonight, will it be white?
Will it be green, or blue, or red?
Will it be the color of blood, the color of war?

Mist of Time

early foggy mornings,
my favorite time…
one can be alone with
memories and tears,

like an ebony black monolithic
serpent the wall stands there,
almost hidden in the fog,

shrouding one's thoughts in
the misty haze of time.

I see images of soldiers moving
from place to place…like me…
stopping to see old friends and
renew friendships.

medals and ribbons left scattered
about before a silent black wall
that stretches to eternity carrying
names of sons, brothers, sisters,
fathers, relatives and friends…
heroes all…here on the wall.

names carefully inscribed,
revealed in the mist of time,
a reminder of the price paid
for freedom.

On Memorial Day

[A Combat Veteran's Perspective]

I have the same flashbacks
every year on Memorial Day.
It matters not if the sun is
shining or if the sky is gray,
The mirage I see is the same…
silhouettes of soldiers I knew
Who died fighting for freedom and
for peace for me and for you!

I get the same eerie feelings
I had fighting the enemy…
A ghostlike enemy that quite
often we never did see
Attacking with a vengeance…
then, usually they would flee
Leaving dead or dying soldiers
bleeding all around me!

I ask God often why I lived
and why my friends died.
I ponder the same thoughts today
yet, still, I just can't decide.
The feeling is much like an
eternal ebbing of the tide
Stirring sad emotions that
are harbored deep inside!

Today on Memorial Day.
we pause to remember
Soldiers that died who will always
be a beloved family member
Symbolized in ceremony
by lighted candles each hold
Honoring their bravery and
the myriad stories untold!

Today brings sadness and
the shedding of many tears
And the inner heartache of
the emptiness over the years.
But today, I also feel very proud
of the soldiers I have known
Because every day I feel their spirit
and I know I'm never alone!

When the Cannons Cease

The guns are quiet now.
The cannons have ceased their deafening volleys.
The battlefield is still…I can see the steam rise from
The bodies of those who lie lifeless against the frozen ground.
I hear the agonizing screams of the wounded
Who still lie scattered all around
As I walk amongst the devastation of humanity.
There are no distinct uniforms,
No recognizable insignias of rank,
Just the soiled, mud-clad garments of warriors.
There are no "victors" here…no "champions of the cause"…
Only the red-stained earth, decorated with the faces of children
Outlined with the motionless frames of young men…Now gone.
The open cemetery before me addresses my soul
With grave irony, and an exclamation in revelation
With regards to the quest for the brotherhood of man.
As the screams of the wounded begin to fade
I am reassured that more have joined their brethren.
Today's carnage will be totaled, and the sum
Of the lives that lay amongst the ruin
Will become a footnote one day…
A footnote that the children, whom these dead will never know,
Read about in a history book, a place unknown to their world,
Just a footnote, a sum total, a collective amount.
As I look around, it's got to be more…
So much more; they all count.
They were all born of flesh, and bone, and blood.
They all died, this day, this place, in this mud,
Each one, each side, they all had a name.
They all had loved ones who must now bear their pain.
It no longer matters for which side they fought.
Right or wrong, their freedom's been bought.

Where Were You?

Where were you when the yellow submarine sailed?
Did your sky sparkle with diamonds?
Was Lucy's face hiding in the clouds?
Did the lucky man make the grade?

Was it the best day in your life?
Did the bus pass you by?
Was the morning coffee the reason why?
Did what you did the year after that make it all less important?

I walked a yellow brick road.
I learned to carry a different sort of load.
I was a boy wearing a soldier's clothes
Marching to where hell was froze.

You said yes, I said no, you said stop, I said go.
I went and said hello to another life.
The old one was left behind.
It was just as well.

The guitar and I gently wept.
It was years before my nights were peaceful and I slept.
I still hear the horrible ringing.
I just pretend the angels are singing.

One day they will be for all of us I suppose.
That is okay.
We all have to board that bus.
That is the last battlefield and nobody can dodge that one.

Three for War

we covered it all some
would say.
three brothers…
three branches…
we don't talk of war or
about those years
each remembers inside…
of losses felt and those
left behind.

medals and ribbons left
at the wall along with
untold tears that never end
for friends and family…
seen only now in our
memories.

Highest Tradition

I am but one of many
Who have served in a fine long line.
So many before have paid the ultimate price
So many more will someday…sometime.
When we raise our hand and recite the oath
To defend and serve till the end,
To the right a stranger, to the left as well,
Soon to become trusted friends.
For many weeks we endure the hardship,
Often grief, and always pain,
But through it all we go together.
Days of sunshine, nights of rain,
If one should fall, then together
United, we all make it through,
For tomorrow one of us may also fall.
Then we'll need extra strength too,
And when we are done with all the basics.
The running around, and all the drills,
We will then be sent somewhere else,
Some far off place, with many hills.
Then with family and friends a world away
We will be caught in some hostile condition,
Shoulder to shoulder we will see it through
In keeping with the Highest Tradition.

Memories

[10/22/68]

Reflections ripple steadily across the surface of the quaint pond
Glistening into the eyes of nature's creatures unseen or beyond
Of a place to reminisce memories of the heart and mind so fond
Touched by early morning dewdrops adorning the fern's frond.
Sounds echo subtly from the splashes made by a fish and a frog
As predator snakes prey on the minnows and a small pollywog
Light rays, both at morning and dusk, leave visitors' eyes agog
Witnessing the pristine growth and life of nature's peaceful bog.

Peace prevails even after the storm stirs the lily-covered water
As a tiny field mouse looks for food like a playful young otter
Watched by lovers above the grassy bank in a leisurely saunter
Enjoying a stroll together with their yet unborn baby daughter.

Now hand-in-hand and hip-to-hip the lovers share deep emotions
Eyes aglow with passion's smile, foretells their intimate notions
Mesmerized by their feelings and fueled by their bodies' motions
As sensual kisses and touches awaken their bodies' silky lotions.

I yearn for these feelings again on grassy slopes shaded by trees
And the sweet fragrance of blooming flowers pollinated by bees
Growing under the forest's branches covered with painted leaves
Yet, in war, my thoughts are nothing more than secret memories.

Shock and Awe

Shock and awe have been used to describe aerial war.
To me those words mean something much more.
They describe what comes over me at certain times.
They tell of my emotions, all bound up inside.

So often I hear stories told by some war's warrior.
I regularly ingest their fear and absolute terror.
What they have done dwarfs my own meager duty.
I am in awe of them no matter their humility.

Emotionally my understanding is the mission.
As I listen I curl up safe in a fetal position.
I have done just enough to see and understand.
My own contribution pales by comparison.

I close my eyes as one tells of incoming rounds.
I can hear him and remember those sounds.
Hot shrapnel flies in the air, dripping blood behind.
The images are here and now in my own mind.

He tells of the voices, screams in the fearful dark.
The pain he recalls is so vivid and very stark.
Calls for medics, bandages, and cursing all delays
Tear at his heartstrings, his nerves are frayed.

I feel with him as he searches for muzzle flashes.
The rounds continue to rain, bombs crashing.
It may be only minutes or even seconds of hell
But the time was eternal as our warriors fell.

It is my hand pressuring the bandaged wound.
My ears hear the blood hitting the ground.
My heart is pounding as fear dictates my pulse.
Let me live one more day is the shouted result!

It is his story but in shocked awe I absorb his tale.
It must be shared and in this I will not fail.
I do not have much to say of what I did back then.
But now I must tell about truly heroic men.

In my few months I did enough to comprehend.
The valor and work of many will never end.
Some died but many lived, keeping history inside.
As long as allowed, their tales I will confide.

In my mind, that fetal position an emotional defense,
I will know where they were and go where they went.
I am safe; it is not me under attack, living in their hell.
I can share their words, feeling what they all felt.

How do you tell about the smell of decaying flesh?
How do you avoid keeping memories this fresh?
How do you tell of the sounds of too late mercy?
Forgetting what they gave will not be my legacy.

Did You Know

lying in the ground
covered by the earth
and fallen leaves
I make no sound.

do I breathe?
none can see
for I am in the ground
lying there without a sound.

a soldier walks by
not seeing me,
for I make no sound
lying in the ground
until I take him down.

do you know
how many faces in the
night that I see?

Purple Hearts

Military soldiers represent all races and all walks of life
Many are single or are married with children and a wife.

Most volunteer for the military ... others answer the call
When Uncle Sam needs men to protect freedom for all.

A soldier knows the meaning of brotherhood and sacrifice.
A soldier puts his life on the line without thinking twice.

Combat soldiers witness death ... the worst of war's hell,
Facing enemy bullets, mortars, rockets, or artillery shell.

Combat soldiers are fearless and tireless when facing death
And more determined when a buddy takes his last breath.

More determined to win so his buddy's death isn't in vain
Fighting the enemy, the environment, and the inner pain.

A combat soldier knows his chance of being hit is very high,
Completes the mission even if it takes more than one try.

A soldier's heart is big, full of courage, devotion, and pride
In country, flag, and helping others with arms open wide.

Wounded soldiers who lived returned to a land of the free,
Know the value of words like honor, peace, and liberty.

Soldiers shed blood for the freedom and the rights of others
Completing their missions in memory of fallen brothers.

This poem honors all wounded soldiers and is meant to impart
Thanks to every soldier who was awarded a Purple Heart!

The Stone

I'm eighteen…it's Christmas Eve
And I can see the lights along the shore.
I'm finally home
It seems so long…
Since I left to fight this war.
I enlisted early
I had to go
For me it was the right thing to do,
Have I regrets?
My heart often cries
For those who didn't make it through.
I'm eighteen…it's Christmas Day
I'm not quite sure what I feel.
I know I am home
Here around the tree.
Somehow it does not seem real,
I feel as though I'm dreaming
Floating high above the ground,
I feel so light…like a feather
And as I am looking down,
I see my dad below me
Next to him I can see my mom,
They are kneeling next to a stone that says
Here lies our son…
Died Christmas Day…
In Vietnam.

The Bunker

Living in the mud,
Protected by the sand,
Too many miles from home
Will it become my tomb?
The Man has us digging
With shovel and hand.
I hate this burlap.
It is some plastic crap.
It scrapes and scratches.
It tears skin off in patches.
The mud is hard to scoop.
My shoulders have drooped.
The weight of the sun
And the burning of mud
Have made my sweat run.
Blisters and some blood,
My hands ache and throb.
My breath comes in sobs.
I have only done a thousand.
Is it waste or a good plan?
Will my life depend on it?
I'd rather gamble on incoming shit.
I could dig a block down.
Stacking it up makes two rows.
I don't need more sand.
My head is a small target.
Doing this every day blows.
The heat, the sweat, the shakes,
The bowed back, the aches…
It never ends and we just
Move on.

The culvert we use too
Is heavy, but the real barrier.
We huddle in it at night
For maybe an hour or two.
Being inside is almost scarier
Than staying close by outside.

We carry that steel, then
Pile more bags on its skin.
It gets taller and stronger
While we only get smaller
And have no sense of belonging.
Salt pills and swallows of bad water.
We still do what we ought to.
Today I filled up in a bomb crater.
My water is a murky blue.
But, it will do…it will do.
We may stay a day, maybe three.
Then we will do what we do.
The more of us close by,
The bigger the thing will be.
We walk; we dig; we may fight.
We will dig in again tonight.
The Claymores will be planted
And we will dig some more.
Even if we don't use it
Somebody else will.
Then we will
Move on.

And do the bunker
All over again…
Then move on.

Open Wounds

I feel the sun coming up…
eyes almost refusing to open.
Dancing fears skitter across closed eyelids.
One more day of life and I am thankful to be,
yet, afraid to face another day.

Steaming jungles, rice paddies, mud-choked
ground; bloodsucking leeches
fill my dreams…my life.

Home! Isn't that where fear does not exist?
Where bullets are not served as dessert?
Where real beds exist or is that my dreams speaking?

It gets tougher to drag myself from my dreams
to a semblance of reality…this reality.
The world looks different through
eyes with open wounds and a
mind UN-healed today…if ever.

Reality

[4/30/68]

Popguns, peashooters
Toy, wooden rifles too
Cap guns, bows and arrows
Fantasy dreams come true.

High school, puppy love
The future is today
Summer job, college days
Books give way to play.

Reality check, the unthinkable
Hits me squarely in the face
War, whether I like it or not,
Raging in a faraway place.

Drafted, in the Army,
A boyhood game of mine
Training, strict discipline
Polishing brass to a shine.

Proud, untried soldier,
A totally different, new me
Scared, feeling lonely
I'm in the airborne infantry.

Home, short leave and tears,
The long flight to Vietnam
In country, the A Shau Valley
And, Twenty-Third Psalm!

Art of War

The art of war,
Such a haunting thought,
To compare as though it were beauty,
Who will be the brush?
Who will be the color?
And who must die to do canvas duty?
What manner of man
Should endeavor to conceive
That death indeed have such form?
Would be simpler to note
That a bird far from home
Would choose to be lost in a storm,
The art let us say
Simply children at play
King of the hill…who is best,
The colors run red
And let it be said
The cost is paid by the rest.

Sounds

As I sat in the quiet, sounds reached my ears.
I was unsure of the source as I shed my tears.
They were faint tones, haunting and distant.
A piano played haltingly, soulfully muted.
From where did they come; why strange to me?
I thought of lost friends; where might they be?

Were they sounds of angels' wings beating the air?
Or were they a ringing of a fork's tines, so unfair?
Was it the sound in my own ears, never muffled?
Whatever they are, my heart is pounding, troubled.
The pulsing at my temples sends shockwaves out.
A throbbing behind my eyes may make me shout.

I look in the mirror but no swelling do I see there.
Yet I think I am ballooning, throttling unseen fear.
The shake of my hands, the quiver in my sad voice
Make me aware that I made another wrong choice.
Living with it is a monster of my own "mis-creation."
Silencing sounds, moving on, is cause for celebration.

Reflections

I have difficulty explaining why my eyes are black mirrors
Reflecting cold images indelibly marked in my mind,
A look referred to, in Vietnam, as the 10,000 mile stare.
But today few people realize this and fewer really care.

I have mused over the years about the events of my life
How the war affected me, memories yet burning inside,
Memories that few, if any, could truly understand
Unless they fought and survived in such a horrible land.

I have lived with the horrors of war I faced in Vietnam
Seeing my buddies wounded then taking their last breath,
Praying that their souls would end up in a better place,
Yet, I am still haunted today by the images of each face.

War is tragic and why combat soldiers very seldom heal.
Their war experiences are mind-altering and so surreal,
Remaining personal and a war veteran's worst nightmare,
Events veterans want to forget…events we rarely share.

I am much older now, to be exact, by forty-one years.
I lie awake reliving the war that still rings in my ears,
Trying to let events go, along with my inner fears,
And although wiser…I still can't stop the flow of tears.

I have often wished that I never had these experiences,
Yet, because I did, I value everything I have even more,
Like freedom, God, peace, and the red, white, and blue,
And explains why I appreciate life more than most do.

Dream in Black

bedtime stories…not the usual…
no Hansel and Gretel, three pigs
or happy endings.

horrors in the mind
of VC hunting GIs while they slept
torment that hindered rest.

as the sun dropped
blackness of night and its fears reared
their ugly heads,

mud-filled foxholes were the Ritz Carltons
of this government-run spa vacation,
all expenses paid for by them…by us.

sounds of gunfire, the alarm clock of 'Nam,
hard not to think of death
but best not to dwell…

no one leaves their memories behind.
fears may ebb
but the haunting never stops.

my dreams are in black,
monolithic in this world's reality
etched forever the names of those we remember.

I have stood at the Wall,
firefights echoing in my mind,
hearing soft footsteps walking by,

and walked away leaving my tears behind
as silent visions of faces remembered
marched through my mind.

Final Muster

Now, as the sun sets high
On this hill that overlooks the sea,
This is the time I am at peace.
The ocean is blue for as far as I can see,
The grass 'neath my feet is well manicured.
It embraces the gardens of stone,
As I stand in awe in their presence
I am surrounded by courage well known.
Each marker, upright in position,
Perfect rows as if standing in Parade,
These, the guardians of our freedom
At final muster where they're eternally laid,
Here in this place…high above the sea,
Each one, at their time, has come.
Now they march through the heavens together
At peace…for a job well done.
If one day you should happen to walk
Through these gardens of stone,
Remember the names that are written here.
Say a prayer for them while safe in your home.
They came from every race and religion,
And on their final day…
Stood up for you…and gave their life
To defend the U. S. of A.

The Sniper

[10/21/68]

Camouflaged and resembling a blanket of leaves
Hidden in the dense, jungle brush and the trees
Positioned just above a winding trail along a ridge
In sight of a tiny but well-used, bamboo bridge…

Ten hours have passed without a single sighting
Instead…soaked by monsoon rains and fighting
Bloodsucking leeches and the mosquito's pain
Frozen…shaking…feeling like I'm going insane…

A sound…damn it all…just a big branch falling
Movement…just what I need…a snake crawling
Heading right for me…it's as big as my thighs
Maybe I can scare it by glaring into its cold eyes.

More movement…voices…can't swallow the lump
Lousy timing, I need to take a leak and a dump
I hear them…but I don't see anything…anywhere
My body is sweating and it itches…everywhere.

There they are…crap…they've got 100mm rockets
Can't help it…warm urine is filling my pockets
Mark the time…the distance…it will take two shots
Aim well…below their funny-looking steel pots.

One, two, three…exhale…slowly squeeze the trigger
The second one looks awkward and much bigger
One, two, three…exhale…slowly squeeze the trigger…I'm done
Damn-it-all, I didn't see him…he's in a dead run…
Body count…three…their blood is soaking the soil
Not much reward for their dedication or their toil.
My crosshairs ended their hopes for continued life
And any chance of ever seeing their kids or wife.
My heart aches…a personal agony…that is daunting.
Cold-blooded acts…the nightmares are haunting.

The sun sets…same war…mentally trying to not bend
My mission…complete…bringing life to an end.

Preparation

A person cannot prepare for life at birth.
One can prepare for death at least.
There are events, once living, that hurt.
How does one deal with that beast?
Some pain is lessened with Preparation H.
Medicine does not soothe all aches.

There are too many things to address in words.
One came to mind that must be said.
It is about a soldier leaving home and hearth.
He or she leaves us; all are afraid.
There is no magic elixir for a time of goodbyes.
The pain of separation is felt on all sides.

The look on a face of one whose life is in serving,
Is etched in the memory of those departed.
Eyes wrinkle at their corners, emotions contorting.
Separation is anticipated with wrenched heart.
Consider the parent holding a child so beloved
When answering a higher call they covet.

The date of leave-taking looms on the horizon.
Dread of that shard has hearts bleeding.
Pain is controlled, longing becomes a prison.
Like water behind the dam, it is seething.
Strength is not only in muscles, never assume.
It must be woven into character's loom.

Duty calls, preparation is done a bit at a time.
It still reminds one there is no good way.
The cost of leave-taking is high, like a crime.
The price paid for the call is only delayed.
Serving one's country is a privilege, it's true.
Its demands cannot be misconstrued.

How do you prepare for a look in a loved one's eyes?
How do you focus on all which might be?
Do you square your shoulders, a smile as a disguise?

Confidence can be worn but is somehow empty.
Everyone is touched by the demands at the higher call.
All give something, others will give all.

All that can be done is to accept the Hand of God.
Do what you must; He is your mightiest sword.
One must march on, life and duty are intertwined.
Whatever the outcome, giving is almost divine.

'Til Now Unwritten

afraid to close my eyes
afraid to die
afraid to live in fear

nothing seems real
in this country called beautiful
~ hellhole to me…to us ~

it never rains here…
sky god just opens the spigot
and drowns everyone…everything

oozing – sucking mud
our sandy beach…
humpin' the boonies…wishing for home

young when we arrived here
we grew old yesterday.
some it took a day, others longer

the sun is watching us again;
comes out to witness death;
theirs, ours, it does not care.

a time of change…
unwritten ~ unwanted…
what I wouldn't give for a hamburger and fries.

The Honored Dead

From the cries at Lexington and Concord
And the battle of Bunker Hill,
The frozen dead at Valley Forge
To Yorktown, where freedom rings still,
America the beautiful, born in Patriots' blood
Bathed in a rich tradition
And blessed by God above,
Our founding fathers forged for us
A declaration by which to live by,
And through the years to protect our freedom
Too many loved ones have fought and died.
Let us not forget our Civil War
Where again for freedom's sake,
For the rights of all in America
And a Constitution we would not forsake,
Each time our country has made the choice
To bear arms and take up the fight,
Our nation's men and women
Have gone bravely into the night.
Remember now the Great War
And three hundred sixty-five thousand strong,
Who were dead, wounded, or missing
By the time the war was done.
Also known as World War I
All the "Powers" got involved,
The war to end all wars they said
But really…what got resolved?
World War II soon beckoned, a dictator in search of a throne.
Foolish were his allies, to ever attack us at our home,
Awakened was the sleeping giant
Again our nation answered the call.
With our allies, side by side we stood
And we watched our enemies fall.
Peace would not remain for long.

The call to arms again filled the air,
Inchon, 38th parallel, and Hill Four-Forty,
Chosin Reservoir, the bravest fought there.
Once again this nation's young fought and died
Once again, we stood firm our ground.
Children still said the "Pledge of Allegiance"
And the phrase "in God we trust" could still be found.
The sixties came, and another war
Again from Indo-China raged,
But this new era of our nation's growth
Would give birth to a different stage.
Law ten fifty-nine, the Tonkin Gulf
And Tet Offensive on foreign shores,
While here at home Jackson and Kent State
Brought the war just outside our doors.
Vietnam, such an unpopular war
Unwanted soldiers at home, and abroad,
Still faithfully they discharged the oath they took
And marched boldly where others had trod.
The eighties, the nineties, and Desert Storm
Our nation revived again.
More blood spilled on foreign sands
By our young women, and men.
911, a terrorist attack
Seeking to instill fear within us all.
Again with courage and renewed strength
We rose up to answer the call,
So stand up straight…stand up with pride
In remembrance, raise your hand to your head,
And with great reverence…give a final salute
To thank…The Honored Dead.

The Wall

Like a broad, grass-covered coastal plain leading to a hidden valley
With a footpath of stone resembling an ancient road or quaint alley
Drawing each visitor to the symmetry of the bunker-shaped mound
Past 140, polished, black, granite, panels rising up from the ground.

Sloped gently from the triangular end panels downhill to the center
Bordered on one side with posts and chain as visitors exit and enter
With lights placed at the base subtly illuminating the panels at night
Truly defining the austere reverence of this hallowed, memorial site.

A 'Directory of Names' is provided near both entrances to The Wall
Listing 58,267 names of the dead who answered their country's call.
Their names etched, five in a row, on 70 panels both east and west
Honoring each soldier who died fighting while doing his or her best.

I visited The Wall first in 1990 then in 2000, and once again in 2001
Each visit a special journey, a personal mission that had to be done.
Having survived the hell of combat unlike many of my close friends
Who felt the agony of pain and loneliness then met such tragic ends.

On my last trip to Washington, I brought the rosters I had obtained,
Names of those I trained with, fought with, and those I had trained.
Nearly 400 soldiers I had known better than I knew my own family,
Yet, I didn't know if they had survived and returned home like me.

I knew of only a handful of my buddies that were killed in Vietnam
But, I had to know what happened to the rest to have an inner calm.
I looked for each name in the directory…in the privacy of my room
And when I finished, 48 hours later, my life was shrouded in gloom.

On day four, I made a rubbing of each name, alphabetically A to Z
And…as I touched each name…I felt my buddies reaching out to me
I returned to my room…physically ill in a serious state of depression
With flashbacks…shaking and sweating…an eerie mental regression.

Unconsciously…I printed the names of my buddies who were KIA
Each on an American Flag I would place at The Wall the next day
I couldn't stop shivering, nor could I stop the steady flow of tears
Having just found out so many buddies were dead after…32 years.

Before sunrise my last day, I solemnly placed the American Flags
At the base of each black panel like I was tagging black body bags,
Then I bid each farewell and saluted true heroes who sacrificed all,
A total of 192 buddies…their names etched on…The Vietnam Wall.

Slaves to a Purpose

We have passion and a purpose.
It controls us while it moves us.

Each day it is a portion of time.
We look for its meaning, a sign.

The message is liquid and flowing.
We learn too, never all-knowing.

There must be a better way, a plan.
We seek strength to make a stand.

We must be a loud voice to remain.
We must guard against the disdain.

We march in invisible formation.
Word travels across this nation.

There is a unity in many efforts.
Each dream is good, deserving.

Veterans, our eternal protectors,
Each facet is for them, sacred.

Each goal, each aim, each purpose
Touches them from all directions.

Each group, working in independence,
Helps the other, does not ever relent.

The plan is divine with mutual respect.
They do not allow their faces to fade.

As long as the purpose lives, strains,
There is hope in our fields of grain.

Heroes All

faces in the fog of history
echoes of empty hearts left behind
fallen ~ but not forgotten.

victories and defeats matter not
only the silenced voices of those
that gave their all.

names ~ most unknown,
these makers of history,
loved and missed by their own.

walking their posts forever now,
all heroes, who gave their all
forever standing tall.

when the flag passes they stand rigid
these soldiers who gave their all,
show them you remember – stand tall with them
as Old Glory marches past.

No Cease-Fire

It seems so long ago
and still just yesterday,
In a place so foreign
And yet, in my own backyard,
I did not know my enemy
And they lived across the street from me.
I fought for those I loved
Those, the same, who condemned me,
When leaving to come home.
A Vietnamese citizen hugged me and wept,
When I finally got home.
An American citizen spit on me,
The Vietnam conflict (war)
Over after 10 years,
The Vietnam Veteran's conflict
After more than thirty-five years
Continues to rage.
All of America offers no cease-fire
Still, no welcome home.
Would I defend Her again?
Damn right, I would!

To a Gold Star Mother

As a mother you never dreamed, though a bit chagrined,
That the child you nurtured, loved, and disciplined
Would leave home without your watchful eye, unprotected
And face the world alone while being subjected
To life's wrath and to mankind's unthinkable wickedness,
Naïvely stating, "I'm going to fix the world's mess."

As a mother you developed your offspring's foundation,
Though some days tears were felt instead of elation,
Yet, lessons you learned and taught helped you resolve
To allow freedom hoping that right would evolve,
But some choices, though tough, left you with little doubt
You might lose your child and be left forever without.

Today we honor your sacrifices and hope you understand
That we are here for you to hold your trembling hand
And let you know your grief is felt from both near and far.

Pain felt and seen by everyone like the brightest star,
An eternal reminder of your sorrow and of your sacrifice,
Knowing your child fought bravely and paid the price.

We honor your love and devotion to a child that is gone,
To the memory of a soldier that sees no dusk or dawn.
We honor you today as an American Gold Star Mother

And ask your forgiveness as we remind one another
That freedom has a price and it cost you a daughter or son
Preserving peace though the battle has not been won.

What of Safe

there is a constant assault from
the darkness on our ears.

each night it grows more quiet...
hard to rest in this paradise called HELL.

snakes ~ VC: both slither in the night;
each in turn looking for a kill.

here on this unknown soil, fighting an undeclared war,
each night voices growing quieter...

fear, anticipation, doubt, and confusion reign
even in the night blood is still red.

dreams, if they come, our escape...
victor Charlie watches.

our unrest obvious, his patience unending,
hoping to quiet the last voice.

My Turn, My Tour

I saw a drawing.
It stirred memories.
The image was life bursting…forth.
The image was death bursting…out.
It was RPGs and mortar shells.
Hell, it was even puppy-dog tails.
It was wading rice paddies with a smile.
It was the pain of trudging another mile.
It was jets screaming across the sky.
It was me asking myself "why."
The image was triple-canopy jungle.
It was booby traps and K-rats.
Hell, it was even just the rats.
It was mortar shells coming and going.
It was me and my guys coming and going.
It was the glow of a lit cigarette in the dusk.
It was a shallow slosh of water erasing dust.
It was an image of my girl floating beneath stars.
Which one? It did not matter, it was one.
It was the face of the girl on enemy radio.
In World War Two she was Tokyo Rose.
It was the foliage around me filled with bugs.
It was the explosion of whistling bombs.
It was the shouts of "Chu-hoi" at battle's end.
It was the last letter my mother sent.
The image was my face in a muddy flowing stream.
It was guard duty intruding on my dream.
It was the muted sound of a stealthy radio playing.
It was the knowledge that it was a game we were playing.
The image was a torn body rolled into a poncho.
It was the whirl of a "medi-vac" on the move.
It was the screams of pain after the tracers flew.
It was an image of the last of all we knew.
It was my turn, my tour, my life, perhaps my death.
But it was an image that hurricanes cannot destroy.
And neither could the years.

Unfaded Memories

ambushes, storms, mud, monsoons, mud…
memories unfaded of Nam.

this is not Hollywood…no scripted stories…
and the all too often happy endings.

no red carpets to walk here…only claymores…
silence a companion, like a silent death.

on point, flank…humpin' through your days,
jungle boots, jungle rot, cries of "medic" heard a lot.

silence broken by screams in the night,
just one more of many bad nights.

time filled with the shadow of death
clock tickin' time, days tickin' by.

soul twisted – heart twisted…
mind a shambles, praying for home.

yes…I have memories, how can I not?
wish time would see them fade…

Put me in, Coach

Coach, I hear there is a new game to play.
The word is it's in Southeast Asia.
It is an unknown place; Vietnam they say.
Is it near the place called Malaysia?
Hey Coach, give me some special training.
Teach me here so I can go, Coach.
I am ready, the time is right so no delaying.
When there, will they share a roach?

I am a proud American and ready to serve.
There is need so politicians say.
Get me ready and I will save some lives.
Helping is the true American way.
The day came and they said I was ready.
A weapon was clean and zeroed.
The Vietnamese dictionary was packed.
I took thirty days and hit the road.

I got off a plane to be greeted by heat.
I checked a map before leaving.
Army taught me, I was ready to teach,
Still a newbie, still believing.
Another education began in the Jeep.
There were soldiers already there.
What they said made me feel weak.
Cynicism was thick in humid air.

The poor people did want our help.
Corruption was their history.
Suddenly I was unsure of what I felt.
Cynicism inflated my worry.
ARVNs and village cops awaited me.
Tactics were clear on paper.
I would teach them how to be free.
That was all I had to deliver.

Weeks turned into months of sweat.
Reporting to different people
Made coaching a hard, hapless task.
Success became impossible.
They issued a weapon but no ammo.
It was truly a FUBAR gig.
Forced failure would screw us too.
Soldiers want to do the job.

Allies laugh at artificial warfare rules.
"Get shot at but do not shoot"
Can only come from noncombat fools.
History is ignored, so we lose.
I was there early; it was in sixty-six.
I came home but went again.
I was sent home again in sixty-eight.
Politicians just refused to win.

I cannot reconcile the stupidity I saw.
It is not the American way.
I walked proud but was made to fall.
Even worse we do it today.
I shared my story for a man to write.
He did not get it all I know,
But he knows, as do all who fight.
We lost our heart, even soul.

Dreams ~ Nightmares

[one and the same]

I see faces in the blackness of my dreams;
voices that sound distant and alone infringe
on my sleep.

waking nightmares filled with the guilt of living
inundate my mind...why them and not me?
did they do something wrong?...did I?

if I told you I have been there
would you understand?... I have not always...
I do now.

there is right and there is wrong.
you and I live in the gray in-between
wondering if peace will come.

what do you see when you close your eyes?
what do you feel when you see faces in the night?
what of the screams...will they ever sleep?

To My Son

[8/20/68-1/23/83]

There are so many things I wanted you to know
About me and the Vietnam War, as you began to grow…
Things that only now your dad understands better…
Things I wanted so many times to write you in a letter.

I wanted you to know I came back a different dad,
Lost and unable to understand the many things I had,
So numb I didn't appreciate you as a young lad
Because my mind was far away, my heart torn and sad.

I still don't understand a great deal about my postwar
Aside from the fact the war cost me my son and wife,
Something I know you couldn't understand in sixty-nine,
When your mom and dad were walking a very thin line.

I wanted to tell you that I cared and that I loved you too,
And how I wanted to take you fishing or to the zoo,
But I wasn't me…I had changed and felt I was in jail,
Thrust into civilization with my mind continuing to wail.

I've lived with guilt and sadness ever since Vietnam,
Knowing I caused hell and unrest instead of being calm,
But it's important that you know I held you on R&R
And your mom sent me your pet rock, knife, and toy car.

I wish I could change things, but I don't have a crystal ball.
And I live knowing the only you I know hangs on my wall.
I miss you, and love you, and my tears don't bring relief…
Instead I live with my mistakes and a Dad's eternal grief.

And because I didn't get to tell you
I love you again before you died…

Poet or Warrior

The question was posed and the answer is known.
Life evolves and
Truth changes when one is grown.
What we did when young was not always by choice.
Some were bold but
Uncle Sam had the loudest voice.
I wrote back then yet I had not the understanding
Of life quite yet, still
I saw, did, and noted what I'd seen.
I was a warrior in a very small way in a small war
That lingers in my mind
And today I try to recall what I did before.
I pulled triggers, dropped rounds in my 81mm tube
When dictated by combat.
That mortar got hot when I ran out of lube.
But was I a warrior? I think so but do not know so.
I never counted if I had kills,
Never saw the faces when they had to go.
That reminds me of something but it is another tale.
I will think about it a bit
Before I search my mind for gory details.
Socrates was a warrior and Plato was a fighter too,
But I am not a philosopher.
People have always done what they had to do.
I walked the rice paddies, slept on those soggy dikes.
I did my tour and my duty.
I somehow lived so today I write.
I am unsure if I was a warrior or if now I am a poet.
I did then what I do now I suppose.
I lived the story then so now I have to tell it.

Heading Home

Today's the day.
Weigh anchor, head for home,
Home, heading home.
Is it possible to go home again?
Is it possible?
To go back to a world now strange to me?
When I left
I was a boy barely seventeen.
As I return
I am a man, an old man at eighteen.
My world is gone…
My innocence, now a casualty of war,
A casualty…
Left on a battlefield with the precious blood,
Precious blood of my brethren.
My eyes now
Will never recognize the childhood innocence
Of my boyhood friends,
Those friends that were closer than kin.
Just a year ago…
A year ago? No, a lifetime ago…
Will their eyes recognize me?
Will they open their arms to me?
Will they beckon me to come home?
Or will they treat me like a criminal?
A criminal convicted of crimes not committed
And encourage me through silence
To continue to search for home?
Heading home…
I am on a ship surrounded by my brethren
Heading home?
I am home…

Not Forgotten

a place barely known to most
faded into the mists of time
where warriors fought and died
where teenagers became adults...

a place that filled minds with ugly scars
for the living to deal with each and every day
la Drang, Khe Sanh, and a thousand
more places unpronounceable...

in hopeless hells fought over for
vague or no apparent reason
where death surrounded you
pounding you down...

a place where sanity never visited
in a war fought with rules
by soldiers on strings...manipulated
who will never forget.

True Americans

Balloons released in the wind
Drift into wide-open spaces
Symbols of American soldiers
Who died in faraway places,

Now but personal memories
On this annual Veterans Day
Remembering what they gave
And the price they had to pay.

Military veterans all stand tall
Proud, never bringing disgrace,
Having fought side-by-side
Without any thought of race.

True Americans step forward
Whenever their country calls.
Veterans never run and hide
Or cower behind foreign walls.

Veterans are true and selfless
Protecting freedom and peace.
Cowards are poor examples,
Poor examples that must cease.

Be very proud of your patriotism.
Be proud you chose to serve.
Be proud you are true Americans.
Such recognition you deserve.

Read at Lafayette Memorial Park Veterans Day Ceremony
Lafayette, LA 11 November 1994

Let Things Go

There may be something running
deeper than the gene pool.
I considered wading in to learn
but didn't want to be a fool.
Each of us has a different type system
For handling a source of pain
And leaving a bad memory's prison.

We have nothing to lose, much to gain.
Some cannot leave it behind,
And swim there again and again.
Some stay while others make brief visits.
Memory draws the moth to the flame.
Mouth drawn tight, some resist it.
We search for courage to let things go.

Life, war and peace, honor and dishonor,
There are things which trap a mind.
It is true misery loves company,
But misery should not be a goal, an end.
I have been guilty of seeking it.
I tell myself to close the cellar door.
My mind becomes an enemy, not a friend.

A meeting of Nam vets has its time of pain.
We all remember the rejection,
That became almost a daily life-thing.
The old embers of anger are always present.
We feed and then cry on each other.
People cannot understand our resentment.
Some ask why and it is a question.

It has always been easy to recall the neglect.
Not much is worse than being a reject.
It is difficult to hear you are a loser.
The lies about us and our effort were abusive.
We lost a war without losing a battle.
Some Nam veterans read those headlines,
Became what they called us, sadly.

We have gatherings of eagles and dogs of war.
Most have the anger in their core.
The difference is whether we control it or it us.
Those who lost the battle need support.
The only comfort they get is in unity.
We go there with them because it has to be.
Everyone wants someone to understand.

My life has been forged by the experience.
Many had their lives defined by it.
I cannot cut myself out of their existence.
I identify with it, yes, I too resent it.
I know they need to let it go.
I know I do too; it would be easier
If some in America were not trying it again.

A friend who cares about me, and also them,
Prays for us all; she served herself.
Her heritage could be worn like an albatross.
She tells me to not forget it,
But deal with it and let things go.
Angst and anger eat the heart of the hater.
She says turn it over to God in prayer.

Between

i find myself stationary
a period of between time

my thoughts propelled by reflections of
feelings
joys
sadness
doubts

our Mother the Earth in turmoil
like our country
green grasses hint at warmth
multi-hued trees speak of death and rebirth

Nam vets stand suspended
between living life
and reliving death

questions unanswered, purpose fading
with the passage of time
sometimes simply disguised for
the sake of a quiet dream…a night of sleep

i marched in a parade of memories
surrounded by my brothers
unspoken each knew we marched
between times

Dear John

I remember my journey home
December 15th…midnight
Full moon…on the equator
Tranquil, calm seas
Warm gentle breeze, tenderly caressing my brow
As I leaned on the rail, port side of the Foc'sle
I gazed into the still hypnotic waves…
I could see her face
Her curly brunette hair
Lying gently atop her shoulders,
I could see her crystal blue eyes
Gazing back into mine…piercing my soul
And so tenderly holding my heart,
I could still feel the softness of her lips
Pressing against mine
An image I had seen every time
I closed my eyes for the last year,
She was the one I ran to
She was the shelter I found at night
When the jungle rain fell hard,
Her arms were the arms that held and comforted me
When my emotions became
Another casualty of the day,
Her hands were the hands I longed to have hold my head
While the cries of fallen brethren
Continued to echo within my mind,
She was the light that guided me home
Safely from every mission,
And she will never know
She will never know, I love her still.

Unscripted

[4/30/68]

I'm on my way to another
world, to another people's land
To fight, protect, hopefully survive,
to lend a helping hand
And give all that I can give
from the little I have and know
Preserving life by taking life
ending life's crimson flow
I'm leaving the only world I know
and those I dearly love
To fight in a foreign country
that knows no peaceful dove,
A nation without harmony,
grieving a steady flow of tears,
Seeing death, knowing more will
die in the coming years.
I'm feeling the apprehension,
it's knotting up deep inside
But in this soldier's mind,
it's a matter of personal pride
Winning the inner battles
for reasons that are mine alone
Unsure of future actions for which
I may have to atone.
Interesting, because I have no known
fears and no qualms,
Yet being in a war is inevitable,
just like my sweaty palms.

Emotion caused by unseen forces
just like an ebbing tide
And under current circumstances,
a little difficult to hide.
Stage left, unseen script,
yet my future role has just begun

With jungle setting surreal doesn't
look like its much fun.
I'll lead by example through
blinding monsoon or hot sun
Praying we're still alive when
the battles are finally won.
I'm here in a foreign world on
another people's homeland
To fight, protect, hopefully survive,
to lend a helping hand.
I'm awake now from my
first nightmare or combat dream
With alarming script, bad vibes,
And a really tragic theme.

A Matter of Trust

Images came to me in the dark of a night.
They were about someone else's firefight.
In a dream I made this trip; it seemed true.
They could be any war and could be you.

The column moves slowly in dense jungle.
Noises are muted and our groans muffled.
Weapons locked, loaded, aimed at intervals.
Sweat runs from strain, physical and mental.

Every move is made, oh so gently, like a lover.
Behind each dark shadow trepidation hovers.
Eyes flickering like the flies that own the bush.
Our breath is shallow, the commands hushed.

The further we walk the deeper is the gloom.
We are on a mission to somebody's doom.
Hissed words, "Stay tight," float to the rear.
Spacing fails, eyes are blind, but we do hear.

Pulses quicken as the back ahead fades away.
Only trouble and blood are brewing this day.
Loneliness is the emotion holding all in sway.
The gaps widen, the situation is far from okay.

Suddenly "A-Ks" are clacking from the front.
Weapons are aimed at the sounds as we hunt.
RPGs start smashing through that green sea,
Yet no ricochets fly through the closest trees.

Our column is split! That is how it has to be.
Now cut off, the front half at Charlie's mercy,
We try to surge forward and things get very hot.
We must get there; our brothers must be caught!

We spread out, but ranks are thinned too much.
The enemy's flank is protected, we have no luck.
Our column can't make way so it is now abreast,
Which is our only choice, but far from the best.

A platoon sergeant yells at us, "Get the hell out.
We gotta call for air support and artillery clout."
A few guys break contact, doing it reluctantly.
Pissed, we do what we must and this has to be.

Silence is forgotten and quick action, the plan.
We have a radio and move out then as one man.
As soon as the din is cleared and the firing faint
"Sarge" dials the radio, calling for an Army saint.

There is traffic; our trapped grunts calling too.
Words are lost in their yells of "we're screwed!"
After getting coordinates move to support's way.
We must bring reinforcements and do it today!

We move quickly, light is not long for the day.
Shadows are sucking sunlight out calling in rain.
It seems forever, but we are challenged to halt.
It is the relief company we so valiantly sought.

We go to the Old Man and are quizzed forever.
We beg him to follow us in a saving endeavor.
"Sir, stop the questions. Our guys are back there.
We don't have the time now; they need our care."

The Old Man says, "We won't charge in jungle dark
It ain't a stroll in New York's Central damned Park.
We move out at dawn's early light, not before then."
"Sir," we chorus, "we gotta go now; they are friends."

"You will not!" was his reply; he meant what he said.
"You go now you won't save them, you will be dead."
As one man we said, "Returning is a matter of trust.
If we do not go now our hearts will sure as hell bust."

The Old Man is right; his words the last to be spoken.
We move in the morning even if our hearts are broken.
"I know men, we have to wait, not just get more killed.
You must trust them to fight, like good soldiers will."

By full light we are deep into the glistening jungle.
Every mind holds to hope that we are saving angels.
The enemy will have a price bloody and dear to pay.
We will save our own and kill Charlie this very day.

Sounds of a hot firefight soon rang in strained ears.
It was not as all-consuming as the evening before.
The guys are alive and it has to be our God's design.
It is a matter of trust; we did come through this time.

Illusive Peace

you – do not hear the screams
feel their pain, my pain
how could you know
you pass me by without a thought
glancing somewhere anywhere, just not at me
I look like you on the outside.
It is the inside you do not and wish not to see.
I came home ~ a place you never left.
I can see into your Hollywood mind
where wounds are makeup and the dead
await their next role.
battles are action and loud noise
cuts and wounds just great special effects.
you can't smell the blood, rotting flesh.
sightless eyes do not haunt you in your dreams.
your friends await you at the local bar.
mine are at peace among the trees,
here among granite slabs and a few last words.
here they find their illusive peace.

What Was I Thinking

What was I thinking, forty years ago?
Just a junior in high school with two proms left to go,
With a championship season fresh under my belt
And big college offers soon to be dealt.
What was I thinking, at sixteen and a half?

Having my mom sign enlistment papers
For me, on my behalf…
What was I thinking when at seventeen, I raised my hand
And took that first oath to protect my homeland?
And in Boot that first morning it was only three…

When that trash can went a ratt-el– ling
I thought…how can this be?
And a voice like a thousand demons…it was Satan, I could tell
When he yelled out "Hit the deck, you worms…welcome to hell!"
My feet hit the floor, my head was still spinning

That nightmare stood there…cigar in mouth just a grinning,
He then shouted out, "You worthless of worthless, worthless of men
Forget all that you know, the lesson's bout to begin,
I am your Company Commander, to you…I am God.

Far better men than you have been where you now trod,
Do not think, speak, or say a word
Just "Yes Sir," and breathing, is all that should be heard,
And I don't want to hear you breathe, let's make that quite clear

For the next twelve weeks I'm your mommy and daddy
not long after that, you'll wish you were still here."
We learned our lessons well, and Ol' Satan Commander
now our friend,

Handed out our orders, as we said our goodbyes
And we prayed we would all meet someday again.
Some got their schools, I was not one…Southeast Asia
was where I was bound.

Ol' Satan Commander was right, his words were so true.
There, the hardest lessons of life, I soon found,
What was I thinking?

Afraid to Sleep

I have had many fears in the dark.
Good dreams are overpowered by the stark.
I have lain down with ears ringing.
I have lain down with my conscience stinging.
I have wept into my pillow silently.
I have remained awake, often diligently.
I have stayed at my post, alert.
I stayed awake to be somewhere first.
I stayed awake with my quaking.
I heard ringing but missed the raining.
I stayed awake to fight pain.
I stayed awake because of the pain.
I stayed awake to avoid dreams.
I stayed awake to avoid nightmares.
I stayed awake to fight too.
My demons come out when I am blue.
I stayed awake to feel my joy.
I stayed awake cursing my fate's ploy.
I am afraid to sleep.
Climbing mountains that are too steep
To face in the daylight
But are no less in the dark of the night.
My pain is real, as is my fear.
If the ringing ever stops maybe I can hear.
I miss the joy of many nights.
Sleeping has become an enigma to me.
I need it for dreams to fly free.

Veterans Day

A veteran is someone, maybe Jonathan or Sue
Who answered the call to protect me and you.
A veteran is someone that decides to serve
A decision that takes grit and plenty of nerve.

A veteran takes an oath that they live by for life
To defend and protect during chaos and strife.
A veteran knows the meaning of being at war
Protecting our homeland or some distant shore.

A veteran knows that freedom has a high price,
Mainly by those who pay the ultimate sacrifice.
A veteran feels the pain of a buddy near death
Or the unforgettable sound of their last breath.

A veteran knows the true meaning of sacrifice
Fighting in jungle heat, sand, or snow and ice.
A veteran has a bond with everyone who serves
And shows each respect that a veteran deserves.

A veteran risks his life unselfishly for others
Protecting each, as though they were brothers.
A veteran deserves respect and the just praise
And for enduring hardships in so many ways.

So, on Veterans Day each year, extend a hand
And thank a veteran for serving our homeland.

Knights of the Night

There is a castle I keep within.
The walls are high and strong.
It is there that I will oft retreat
When I sense that things are wrong.

I will ride my steed across the mote
And draw the bridge up tight.
I'll walk the walls back and forth
Ever vigilant throughout the night.

I will peer deep into the darkness
To find the enemy there within,
Then strategize the best defense
And await the battle to begin.

If needed, I will summon forth
My knights to stand by my side
When they receive my beckon cry
Upon steeds of steel they will ride.

Sir Elavil, Sir Librium,
Sir Valium, and Stelazine,
These are the knights to my aid do ride
To slay dragons that assault my dreams.

Thin Wall

Their rooms are warm,
Some border on hot.
One of the common traits I've found,
Of those not sure
Where, or who they are,
Some say they're mentally unsound,
They live sometimes
Between two worlds
And both at times seem unfair,
So many withdraw.
They hide deep within
In a place that they won't share.
The walls they build
So often close in
They see demons behind each stone,
Their mind is sure
Demons do exist
And they must face them all alone.
But now and then
They seek out the help
That doctors try to provide.
They try to talk
Or prescribe the meds
That often, drives them further inside.
What is it really?
That we medicate
Person, problem, or the signs?
Does it work?
Does it really help?
Or simply numb the mind.

Sleeping with Ghosts

What do we lie next to every night in slumber?
In the quiet dark do our hearts beat like thunder?
Often my eyes close and I see my soul staggering.
There is a ball and chain nearby; hear it dragging?

When we lie down at night we are not alone.
Our memories and mistakes are also in the home.
They are in bed next to us, heads on the pillows.
They linger in the night's fog like weeping willows.

The shadowed figures in the dank of the night
Lurk on the periphery of consciousness and light.
They are indistinct but real, moving but motionless.
They nag, whispering so shrilly, interrupting our rest.

Bones in the closet are like the willow's branches.
They rub together but unseen in the mist, only felt.
The sounds are sensed more than heard at times.
They grate on the nerves, becoming beleaguering.

Skeletons from our lives follow us forever it seems.
They haunt when we try to wrap ourselves in dreams.
Sleeping with ghosts is done by many, sadly it is so.
Accept, face them, march on; you have paid the toll.

Look to the sun in the morning and angels in the night.
The willows are not haunting, the shadows give us fright.
The bones rattle but cannot really harm those of flesh.
Our living spirits can defeat them if we give it our best.

Flag Day

Protecting you and me began when our forefathers secured our freedom, defined and established our Constitution and our Bill of Rights, and fought valiantly for the 'independence' of the United States of America.

Respect takes so little effort, yet for centuries, I've been abused, desecrated, neglected and even threatened. I've braved the wars our soldiers fight today and the many wars our military veterans valiantly fought where I, too, was battle weary, faded, and sometimes full of holes.

Always, I will embrace the profound sadness with dignity and honor, as I drape the caskets of America's Fallen Heroes ... those who have died and those that continue to die protecting you and me so we will remain free.

You see me now, as a reminder that our nation's unity, our freedom, and our peace have all been preserved and protected by our soldiers and veterans. When you see me, show me the respect that I have earned. When you see a soldier or veteran, take time to thank them for the sacrifices they have made!

Honey, Me and My PTSD are Home

like me you can't wait, looking forward to you
a hug, a kiss, a home cooked meal

no cravings, nothing special for me
perhaps fried chicken served between my fits of rage

I want so much to hold you tight
my anger does not care

I want you to know it is not fair…but I cannot share

will I smile when first we meet, see my new son the first time
or cry in the sun, images of charred children clouding my eyes

I have come home to you and he

wondering…can I ever escape the pain tattooed on my mind

It Don't Mean Nuthing

Your walking along talking with your best friend
Then bursts of gunfire, explosions…it feels like the end.
"CORPSMAN!" You hear; it rings within your ears…
You turn to your buddy…to see your worst fears,
Again the cry "Corpsman," comes from another place.
You quickly look round to find the requesting face.
You reach the first fallen, with pieces now gone…
You can't stop the bleeding, won't be very long;
You turn and you follow, the cries, there are many.
No safe place now, you quickly check, there aren't any,
Another one down, you hope you're in time.
It seems they have numbers, so many in line,
And just when you think at least this one goes home.
Another quick burst from the enemy…no mercy is shone,
You have done your best, all that you can do…
You pray you can save one, before the fight's through,
You patch, you wrap, you do your best and then
More explosions, gunfire, and it starts over again.
At the end of the mission, when you're back at base
You sit for awhile and remember each face.
You try to find a place where you can't be seen
And you shed the hard tears, for what has just been,
Each person who died there, to you, deserve the "Button"
You dry your tears, return to work…and tell yourself
"It don't mean nuthing"…
But it does…it does…and it always will!

Silence

Sometimes we sit in silence.
Perhaps that should never be.
The quiet can surround you like a shroud.
Silence adds to the smallest of doubts.
Ideas, best buried, can burrow out.

Fears conquered come back around.
Thoughts denied can charge in like brigands.
Fleeting weakness comes a-storming.
Decisive strength disappears in despair.
Self-doubt patiently waits to reappear.

Those quiet demons can weigh in heavily.
That is not a question, it is certainty.
Sounds you learned merge with the dark.
Things unbidden become abhorrently stark.
Self-recrimination is a shovel digging a grave.

Peace is the body that often lies entombed.
Soul searching finds evils often undeserved.
Silence may challenge the will to live.
Silence combined with darkness has pain to give.
The effects are all too easily observed.

Remember these things too.
Silence can percolate creativity, never forget.
One can retreat to it, controlling unseen forces,
And use them to great advantage, of course.
Meditation is one form and sages place value there.
Do not wear the shroud of silence, but don the cloak
Of wiser minds who learned not to fear the dark.

Just Stopped By

I just stopped by today.
Just wanted to chat to
some old friends and family,
not much to say, but it feels
good to share memories.
My cousin was there, no
surprise, he is always there.
Saint Patrick's Day is his
birthday and I missed it;
we had a bad snowstorm.
No cake…no candles, just a
simple "Happy Birthday."
I let them all know I would
be back; I did not have to say
it, I know they know I will.
I turned slowly and walked
away from Panel 56E,
Line #10, he is always there
same spot forever,
on "The Wall."

jim greenwald served in the Navy in a variety of capacities. "Join the Navy and see the world," whether you want to or not. It provided an opportunity to see much of the world and to meet two presidents. He holds degrees in Computer Science, Business Administration, Business Management, and a Masters in Human Resource Management and Industrial Relations. He is happily divorced, his three children quickly growing older than he, and has four beautiful teenage granddaughters. He is a two-time survivor of cancer who enjoys each and every vertical day, crediting the Creator and a positive attitude for his survival. His writing is a reflection of his multicultural background: Ojibwe, French, and German. He has been a professional photographer for many years who now takes pictures almost exclusively at Native American powwows.

His poetry has been published extensively in e-zines, magazines, and anthologies here and internationally. He has published nine books of poetry to date mixing emotional poetry and Native American oriented poetry and stories; he co-authored a volume of Native poetry and stories. He has received several awards for his writing, including three gold medals from the MWSA for his books titled *Twisted Tongues*, *Tears for Mother Earth*, and *Across the Bridge*, four Editors Choice awards from the International Library of Poetry and two Honor Scroll Awards from Angels Without Wings Foundation, Inc. He is a lifetime member of the Military Writers Society of America, Canadian Federation of Poets, American Authors Society, Academy of American Poets, and the Native American Rights Fund. He lives by a quiet stream in the middle of nowhere in Bedford County, PA where he can hear the water speak.

Michael D. Mullins is a graduate of Clinch Valley College of the University of Virginia (now U. VA, Wise). He earned his undergraduate degree with a major in English in 1974 after serving in the U. S. Army. He later completed an Associate's Degree in Operations Supervision at Indiana University, Kokomo, Indiana.

Mullins has worked in production, inventory control, and human resources management. Between stints in industry, the State of Indiana employed him in its Department of Commerce, where he eventually became the liaison with the Federal Department of Housing and Urban Development. Mullins was a Team Leader for a major automotive manufacturer. For a short time he was a small business owner, as a human resources consultant.

He served his community in many capacities, primarily working with youth-oriented organizations. He was a member of his local board of school trustees for sixteen years and a co-founder of that school's Citizens Scholarship Foundation.

In March of 1968, Mullins was assigned to the Republic of South Vietnam as a soldier in the 199th Infantry Brigade. He served proudly with other young men fighting for this country as an infantryman in combat. He was awarded the Purple Heart for wounds received in action during September of that year. He returned home in March of 1969 as a young man who had seen and learned much. His most vivid learning experience was still ahead of him. The experience led to his award winning book, *Vietnam in Verse: Poetry for Beer Drinkers*, in 2007, which earned the Gold Medal for poetry from the Military Writers Society of America.

Mullins married in 1970 to a woman who has tolerated him ever since. Now he is the proud father of two sons and four grandchildren. They are tired of hearing his stories and are ready for him to share them with somebody else.

J. R. Jellerson is an international award-winning author/poet, singer, and songwriter who has been writing music and poetry for more than thirty-five years; he says that writing helps to keep him balanced and maintain a good perspective on what this life has to offer. His published works have appeared in over sixty countries; he has published over one-hundred songs, recorded five music albums, and written several books. In March of 2009, he competed in the VA Creative Arts Competition; he received Gold Medals in the state wide competition in two categories featuring his music and poetry.

He represented the state of Hawaii in the National Competition, receiving the silver medal for his poetry. In October of 2009, he received the gold medal for his music CD titled "Goin' Home." He also received a silver medal for his book of poetry titled *Poems of Passion and Songs for the Soul*.

In addition to his music CD and book awards, he was also selected as a MWSA People's Choice finalist for the lyrics to his song "Freedom Isn't Free," a patriotic tribute that will be included on his album "Sailing Away."

He enlisted in the Navy at the age of seventeen to become a corpsman. He was a police officer who became a chaplain; he is also a nurse who specializes in ER/Trauma. James is a member of Vietnam Veterans of America and a member of Disabled American Veterans. Currently, he is a "Veteran that serves other Veterans" within the Department of Veterans Affairs Healthcare System.

Lloyd A. King was born in Batavia, New York on March 26, 1944 while his father was on a B-29 Bomber during World War II serving with the United States Army Air Corps, Randolph Field, Texas. Lloyd graduated from Sweetwater Newman High School in 1962, attended Philadelphia College of Art majoring in Industrial Design with a minor in Fine Arts.

After college, Lloyd was drafted into the United States Army in 1967 where he was trained and graduated Basic Infantry Training, Advanced Infantry Training; Airborne Jump School; graduating sixth in his class at the Non-commissioned Officer Combat Infantry Leadership School, and was stationed at Ft. Lewis, Washington, as a Drill Instructor teaching Advanced Infantry Training, when he received his orders for Vietnam in March 1968.

During the Vietnam War, Lloyd was a highly decorated combat infantry leader receiving the Silver Star for gallantry, the Soldier's Medal for a noncombative act of heroism, the Bronze Star for meritorious action and bravery, and two Purple Hearts among twenty-one other individual and unit awards, medals, and decorations while serving with Bravo Company, 2nd Battalion, 327th Infantry Regiment, 1st Brigade, of the 101st Airborne Division-Airmobile from 1968 through 1969.

Lloyd re-enlisted in the United States Army Reserves in late 1986, graduated second in his class at the Army Recruiting School and served as an Army Reserve Recruiter stationed in Geneva, New York from 1987 through 1990. While recruiting for the Syracuse Recruiting Company and Battalion, Lloyd again distinguished himself as a soldier, receiving numerous Army Reserve NCO of the Quarter awards, was selected Top U.S. Army Reserve Recruiter and selected as the Top Non-commissioned Officer receiving the distinguished NCO of the Year Award in 1988.

Following his second Honorable Discharge in 1990, Lloyd returned to the oil and gas industry until his retirement in 2003 after a total of twenty-five years of service. Lloyd and his wife, Paula Breaux King, currently reside in Lafayette, Louisiana. In 2005, Lloyd completed pen and ink drawings to compliment the poignant, poetic, stories about some of the many combat experiences he had that were penned by flashlight or moonlight in the jungles of South Vietnam. His book, *From 'Nam With Love*, and published in 2006, was awarded the Military Writers Society of America, 2006 Gold Medal Award for Best Book of Poetry.

Lloyd is a lifetime member of the American Legion, Military Order of the Purple Heart where he is Commander, 101st Airborne Division Association, Am-Vets, Disabled American Veterans, Veterans of Foreign Wars, and the Vietnam Veterans of America. Lloyd continues to write about Vietnam and his powerful writing style, as found in *Kings of the Green Jelly Moon*, continues to touch the hearts and souls of those who read his writing and see his artwork.